CAN I
FRANK?

CAN I BE FRANK?

Poetic Insights that Empower and Inspire

FRANK PASCIUTI, Ph.D.

Illustrations by Craig M. Linderman

Cover and interior design by Frame25 Productions
Cover art by Midjourney and Jonathan Friedman

ISBN: 979-8-218545-28-4

PLEASE NOTE: It is the author's hope that these poems will be helpful to readers in support of emotional and mental well-being. If any poems speak to you particularly, and if you would like to reproduce them either for friends or family or as a therapist, please do so but also credit the book as their source. Thank you.

—Frank

You may contact the author via email at
frankmarcpas@gmail.com

CONTENTS

To Jane

for her many years
of love and support

INTRODUCTION

Do you recall an occasion when a parent, teacher, mentor, or coach may have passed along an encouraging saying or proverb that perfectly applied to what you were facing in your life at the time? They may have stated something like, "This too shall pass," or "You reap what you sow."

Maybe it was an analogy that captured your situation, or a fitting metaphor that stuck with you over the years. When it's recalled, it may bring back thoughts of how it pertained to your life then, or even now.

Many psychotherapists use similar analogies and metaphors to empathically capture the essence of what a client may be expressing, or to enhance insight into the overall focus of their therapy.

For example, in my decades of conducting therapy, I frequently tried to help people become more aware of their feelings at a given moment, how they can become more mindful of them in the middle of an interaction, and how that present awareness can guide them to respond in real time. I refer to this as "feeling on your feet."

This book of rhythmic, rhyming, and reflective poetry was constructed to serve a similar purpose. But it consists of more than just one liners or brief proverbs. The majority of these poems are literal, direct, and easily accessible, unlike most poetry, which requires effort to just unpack what the poet/poem is actually saying. What requires thought with these poems, which cover a variety of subjects, including feelings, thoughts, relationships, perception, and spirit, is how the meaning or explicit points made in each one may have relevance to you or someone you know.

If a poem inspires a deeper search for self-understanding, you may wish to look at the book I wrote from which these poems were distilled: *Chrysalis Crisis, How life's Ordeals Can Lead to Personal and Spiritual Transformation*. Or, if desired, you may wish to seek out some counseling.

Irrespective of any need for further reading or professional aid, I believe you'll find the poems provide food for thought, and their structure, illustrations, and information, insightful, and enjoyable.

—Frank

A POET WARRIOR

It came to me at fifty-three, *my* pen could be a sword.
I'd be a poet warrior, use words to cut the cords
of people bound by endless
quests to solve their discontent,
all hoping they'll find happiness
in how their money's spent.

I'd write of how they bind themselves
with all those golden chains.
Like mindless cattle moved en masse,
herded toward new claims,
by ads that say they'll sell them
goods assured to make them whole.
I'd write of ways to fill those voids
which would not take a toll.

I'd write of mindful practices;
they're free and give you peace.
How using them can satisfy, how craving can decrease.
How they unite us all as one, how we can find true home.
How having that experience, we would feel less alone.

Yes, I admit it's grandiose to think with just my pen,

that I could help distracted

souls find peace in life; but then,

it is a way I can suggest a path that we are told

can still our mind and calm our soul,

free us from karma's hold.

BEING FRANK

When we need to be direct and broach what must be said,
If spoken diplomatically, we may not be misread.
Because when said with tactfulness, it's easier to hear.
Emotions can be managed well,
and meanings can be clear.

But even if directed well, what's shared may be ignored;
Like water off a ducklings' back, it can pass unabsorbed.
When someone lacks the readiness to take in what we've said,
while our ideas have worthiness, few penetrate their head.

However, when appropriate, we still may want to seed
the thoughts we feel must be expressed,
despite where they may lead.
You never know which land on rock, and which hit fertile soil,
but someday you may come to find
that growth came from your toil.

So say what you feel must be said, be clear while being kind,
and optimize the outcomes of results you hope to find.

IT STARTED WITH A CRISIS

It started with a crisis arising in his life.
When he was told what had occurred it felt as if a knife
was driven deep into his heart. He stood in silent shock.
His legs began to falter, as though the ground did rock.

At first he couldn't focus, not knowing what to do,
initially denying what occurred was even true.
But soon reality set in and then from deep inside,
a wave of strong emotion rose, and suddenly he cried.

That ordeal led him to a path he thought he'd never walk,
where he set out to find someone to listen and to talk.
He spoke about that crisis, and some others he'd repressed.
His heart was broken open now, and though he tried his best

the feelings of those older hurts no longer stayed inside.
They surfaced to awareness from the places where they lied.
Like lava through volcanic vents, the fissures in his heart,
allowed those feelings to come through and let the healing start.

And once his feelings got diffused, the old ones and the new,

he felt transformed, lighthearted now, in ways he never knew.

To self-reflect and look within was something he'd ignored.

Engaging in such practices he thought was self-absorbed.

And though this life ordeal caused pain, he now can clearly see,

why many say that crisis offers opportunity.

FEELING ON MY FEET

You ask me how I'm feeling now.
I think as I delay.
I'm just plain stumped, and don't know how
I feel or what to say.

You claim that knowing feelings
can guide me when I need.
A compass which can point out paths
where thinking might not lead.

You say with work I could get clear
and someday, in a beat,
when asked my feelings quickly share
what I feel on my feet.

RUNNING MEDITATION

Long distance running can be a retreat,
like still meditation, but done on your feet.
It's able to gain what's achieved Buddha style,
but rather than sitting, acquired after miles.
As senses get filled and expanded by motion,
where regular breathing, like waves from the ocean,
combine in a rhythmic entrainment with stride,
and lead to a trance that will turn you inside.

DAYS OF HEAVEN

If we want days of heaven's' bliss,
they can be had by doing this:
Master the ways of how we grow
in ten key areas that we know.

When they're all grown sufficiently,
we'll live our lives in harmony,
experience a peace profound,
and find more joy and love around.

The first key asks that we take care
to mind our health and be aware
of how we can responsibly
provide what's needed *physically*.

To learn more *intellectually*
will help us think more critically.
It's key to what's believed or thought,
so we can grow from what we're taught.

The next key states that we should *feel
all our emotions*, which reveal
what's in our heart, and helps us be
more capable of empathy.

And if we carry any guilt
about past deeds, and find they've built
a sense of shame we feel inside,
let *moral* absolution guide.

And as we grow we'll come to see
we form a self-*identity*.
But it may change as we grow more
and shift around while we mature.

Yet when it's clear, we'll feel at peace,
especially if self-doubts cease,
and be inclined more easily
to build relations *socially*.

As some of those relations grow,
we might take risks and let them know,
our feelings and our thoughts within,
more *intimately* let them in.

Then as we move through life we'd be

inclined more *existentially*,

to find more meaning in each day,

with purposes that light our way.

But if one dark night that light died,

and our five senses fail to guide,

then *intuition* is the key

that when developed helps us see.

As these nine keys evolve and grow,

then *spiritually* we'll come to know,

we're more than just what's physical.

We're all multidimensional.

And then when all ten keys are known,

each one attended to and grown,

their synergy helps us realize,

The days of heaven as our prize.

YOU'RE NOT WHO I ONCE MARRIED

"You're not who I once married,"
incessantly refrained,
repeatedly delivered,
accompanied with blame—
that I had somehow fooled you,
and led you to believe
I'd be the one who's perfect,
and now you feel deceived.

I never was that person;
it's you who misconstrued.
You made me your projection,
conceived of, then pursued.
You now act like I planned it;
I baited then I switched,
first I met your every need,
then stopped once we got hitched.

But we can still stay married,
if tolerance is found.
We both have imperfections,
and yet our love is sound.
So strengthening our union,
requires what we do,
is learn to love each other
with our warts and assets too.

A PATH WITH FLOW

To seek a path with purpose
and with meaning you may find,
there are existential questions
circling through your mind.
But only you can answer them,
and you must feel you're free,
to choose the path that's right for you
that others may not see.

It's a sometimes-lonely process,
which you will understand,
that takes some incubation time
before that path's in hand.
And when you do consider one,
revealing what can be,
make sure it meets your interests
and its value's plain to see.

Does it also call for talents
and strengths that you possess?
Then it may be authentic,
which will bring more happiness.

And when you're undertaking
its activities you'll know,
because while you're engaged in them,
you'll function in a flow.

WHO I AM

He turned and in a friendly voice he asked me
who I am.
I could have quickly said my name—
it wasn't an exam.
But I took pause and gave some thought
to my identity,
because that question's crossed my mind
a lot more recently.

Who I am has gotten lost and gnaws
at me these days.
A woman, mother, someone's wife,
I function in those ways.
But in addition to those roles,
inside I'm being urged,
to add to those identities,
have something new emerge.

So meeting a new person is a time
where I can try,
to be somebody different,
and to see if it will fly.
He doesn't know my name yet,
nor does he know my role.
It offers opportunity to
try out something bold.

I could say that I'm single and
I'm playing in a band.
Or I'm a trust fund baby who's
traveling the land.
But then again, I needn't lie,
I'll shake his outstretched hand,
then go ahead, and just for now,
I'll say my name is Anne.

A WATCHED POT

Your anger's like a lidded pot of water on a fire.
When you're annoyed and get upset,
its pressure becomes dire.
You steam, then feelings overflow, in waves you can't contain.
Then lacking rationality, you start to feel insane.
Your unchecked anger turns to rage displayed for all to view,
and afterward with shame you feel how wrong it was to do.

So rather than return the lid again to fasten down,
don't you agree it's time to learn another way around?
Let's try to build a lid that slides and moves aside more free,
that goes from shut to semi sealed and opens by degree.
As pressure builds it then could vent in increments more tame.
Then with your rage of less concern, we can address the flame.

AN OCTOPUS TURNED UP

When you've got buried issues remaining unresolved,
their impacts can affect you until their problem's solved.

Not knowing their existence and being in the blind,
they're like a turned up octopus hiding in your mind.

Its tentacles can infiltrate the many ways you live,
your work, your health, relationships, and the love you give.

Once issues get identified, and rooted at their core,
when remedied and rectified, they'll trouble you no more.

All the ways they influenced your life will then be ceased,
with areas held in their grasp loosened and released.

So If an octopus with issues lies within your mind,
Its problematic tentacles give clues to what you'll find.

IT'S HARD TO HUG A PORCUPINE

You're acting like a porcupine,
you poke, and prick, and pinch.
And when I reach to help you,
your recoil makes me flinch.

If I try to talk to you,
your words push me away,
and filled with hurt and anger,
you snap at what I say.

Did I upset your feelings
when we last had a row?
There must exist a reason,
I'd truly like to know.

Do unexpressed emotions
explain why there's this wall?
Cause if I did offend you,
I'd like to hear them all.
But should you not express them,
or what it is you need,
then future reconnection,
is not where this will lead.

Yet if you laid your quills down,
and chose to work this through,
we could get by this impasse,
and have our hugs renew.

PLEASE LET ME IN

Why are you afraid to open up and let me in,
and share some of your secrets, or how your life has been?
Does it frighten you to think that once inside I'll see
thoughts and feelings that I'll judge,
which you must hide from me?

You're quick to share your thinking about the days' events,
and don't refrain from telling me how your day was spent.
And when I'm lacking knowledge about a needed fact,
you're generous with what you know and teach me what I lack.

But these are all safe topics, and easy to be broached.
The kind of openness I seek, the kind that can't be coached,
requires being vulnerable and risking to reveal
thoughts that are more intimate. They'll deepen how we feel.

If you would try to take such risks, I won't be like a bull,
who rumbles through the closet of your heart when it is full,
trampling tender feelings that you've long sought to protect.
With empathy, not judgement, I will listen with respect.

I hope you'll open up your heart and trust me to come in;
I long to feel the closeness that I know we crave and when
we get to those sweet moments, and we feel them in our heart,
we'll have a deeper love than now, and never want to part.

DAMN THOSE TEARS!

He shut them down, those crying tears,
like capping off a well.
When life dealt him some sad events
his heart could only swell.
He got so full he'd nearly burst,
but never let them flow.
And over time when they'd arise,
he wouldn't even know.

Appearing strong, unbreakable,
a man who's made of steel.
If other's sad emotions flowed,
they weren't the ones he'd feel.
He'd stand there with a poker face,
a real-life Mr. Spock;
he'd offer no compassion
show the softness of a rock.

But then one day the motherlode
of sad events occurred.
Someone he loved was gone for good,
and then his vision blurred.

He fell into a panic
for things he could not see.
The fear got overwhelming,
a threat he couldn't flee.

He tried to gain composure
and eradicate the fear,
but he could tell that didn't work,
he felt like death was near.
The feelings overwhelmed him,
a tidal wave they seemed,
an internal tsunami,
a nightmare never dreamed.

Despite his best defended ways
to clench and grit his teeth,
he burst into a passionate cry—
It gave him great relief.
With further help he also learned
when modulated right,
that letting all his feeling flow,
can even bring insight.

Not giving into feelings,
he thought gave him control,
but now he sees those shut down years
had taken quite a toll.
The feelings that he tried so hard
to not experience,
deprived him of a richer life,
that came at his expense.

Our tears come for a reason,
it's just a simple fact:
It does far more harm than good
to hold those teardrops back.

LET PASSION FLOW

Feelings we have cannot be dismissed
even though we may wish that they could.
Holding beliefs they're best to resist
can raise guilt from just thinking we should.

Avoiding what's felt by distractions,
or addictions that help us take flight,
we'll find that despite their attraction,
that our feelings still wake us at night.

Unconscious feelings lie in the back
of our heart when they've not been diffused.
Compulsive habits leaves them intact
which may strengthen and lead to abuse.

In time, we'll find they're taking a toll
which can feel like we're being possessed.
If we trust we're not losing control,
we'll find peace when they're finally expressed.

Lets not lead life imprisoned by fear.
Lets rid anger that's roiling below.
Purge the sadness that's so hard to bear,
and allow joy and passion to flow.

HOW DO YOU SEE IT?

The reason we see so divergently
results from two types of perception.
One type tends to focus more on the tree,
the other the forest's direction.

Neither type's better. Both have their own view.
But each type thinks what they see is right.
All of us favor the lens we look through,
and show preference for what's in our sight.

When we are biased, and we're not aware,
we're inclined to see myopically,
that what we're viewing is all that is there,
not aware that there's more we could see.
One type relies on what senses reveal.

The other intuitively sees.
Sensors believe their perceptions are real.
The intuitors see what could be.

All our five senses can serve us the best
when we're detailing physical facts.
Intuitive sight imagines the rest
and surpasses what our senses lack.

Each type has its strengths,and when they're allied,
can give full scope of what is perceived.
When jointly employed, they both can provide
that the fullest account is received.

DO YOU BELIEVE?

Bill walked in my office, though that's not his name.
It's cloaked to protect him, but facts are the same.
He sought out some counseling for help with his fears.
When shared with some others, they fell on deaf ears.

It soon was apparent why he'd not been believed,
because what Bill told them was hard to conceive.
It all sounded crazy like he lost his mind.
And though they were leery, they weren't unkind.

Bill told them of dreams where he could foresee
events that would happen and how they would be.
One which was well known, Bill shared in advance.
A friend had confirmed it. This wasn't by chance.

Bill then had two more dreams of family back home,
where he knew some would die before it was known.
This all made Bill frightened, and with bated breath,
he told me he feared he's the angel of death.

Bill wasn't aware of the capacity,
for precognitive thoughts, nor how they could be.
When he heard that he exhaled, and I came to find
he wasn't pretending and had a sound mind.

He later revealed that he once nearly died
from an accident which he viewed from outside
his unconscious body laid out on the ground,
attended by rescuers gathered around.

The near death experience just had become
described in a new book, among which were some
of the NDE features Bill also shared,
and after he read them his fear disappeared.

Much later through research what first was unknown,
was that after an NDE it was shown,
along with the features we know well today,
that psychic capacities surface and stay.

MR. RIGHT LEFT

He loves me, he loves me not.
It's hard to say, he's cold and hot.
I can't quite get consistent reads.
He acts so loving when he needs.

But then there's times when he'll resist
my brief attempts to seek a kiss.
He seems too bothered to respond,
and acts like he's been put upon.

I wonder if it's good for me
to chase his love, or if he'll be,
another man who wastes my time,
and then one day I come to find,

it wasn't love he really felt,
just something said so I would melt.
Then I'd play into his hands
where he would carry out his plans.

And like the others it would end,
with lonely nights where I would spend
my time attempting to explain,
how I'm back in that place again.

He's not the first guy I've pursued,
because I fell for how he wooed,
then quickly let him have his way,
believing in his arms I'd stay.

But now I realize I should slow
the courting process till I know,
that he who seems like Mr. Right,
is not revealed in just one night.

TRIVINI

Your mind, body, and soul
together make you whole.
And when they're synergized,
can also make you wise.

Because if with your will,
you learn to make them still,
you'll find their confluence
awakes an inner sense.

And then you'll come to see,
that all eternity
will open to your eyes, revealing
that which lies within and all around:

a
consciousness
unbound.

BE A THINKER, NOT A STINKER

Be a thinker, not a stinker.
at those times when you might think your
high emotional reactions
create toxic interactions.

If your beliefs make you react,
they need more thought before you act.
You just may find that they're the cause;
when reconsidered, you might pause.

Don't let wrong thinking be the tail
that wags the dog and makes you feel
all out of sorts, and so upset,
that you say things which you regret.

MY HUMBLE TELESCOPE

I set my sights on inner space,
that region of our mind,
where it is said so much exists,
to seek what I might find.

I've heard an inner vision
will enable me to see,
a view of cosmic consciousness
that's beheld consciously.

I'm told it's vast and like the stars
that fill the nighttime sky,
it stretches toward infinity,
beyond what meets the eye.

I humbly ask that I perceive
some part of what may be,
and understand the scope
of that which is revealed to me.

A GRUMPY REMEDY

I saw a man with more than me.
It seemed his life was blessed.
And then I felt some jealousy,
and in my thoughts expressed:

Life's so unfair! He has so much,
and I'm just getting by.
With folks like me he's out of touch.
There's nothing he can't buy.

I also saw a man who's life
was filled with hurt and shame.
I figured he deserved his strife.
He brought down his own name.

Another man is in the news
and seems so virtuous,
a saintly good-y two shoes,
who makes me feel disgust.

And hearing politicians' spin
the lies that I disdain,

I hear myself just shouting out
"you're greedy and you're vain!"

But then I realized suddenly
when thinking in these ways,
I get depressed and tend to be
so grumpy on most days.

I try to now feel happiness
for people doing well,
compassion for those having less,
who's lives may feel like hell.

To learn to trust the virtuous,
and see how selflessly,
they give so much to all of us,
and do so lovingly.

I've learned to not give rogues free rent
to occupy my head,
nor waste the thoughts I could have lent
to other things instead.

I now work trying to reframe
the way I see what's viewed,
and found that it's a remedy
that heals my grumpy mood.

TURNING THE OTHER CHEEK

Sometimes I have to turn the other cheek to truly see,
what lies behind your anger is not always clear to me.
When I'm faced with heated words they're scary and intense.
My instinct is to shield myself and mount a strong defense.

In the past I tried to find solutions you could use,
to fix the situations where you thought you saw abuse.
And due to my discomfort, I hoped those would suffice,
to quell your tense emotions, get you back to being nice.

But now just like a lightning rod I take your angry flow,
I let it pass down through me, and then I let it go.
And often once it dissipates a softer side's revealed,
where underneath your anger, old hurts have been concealed.

While listening with empathy I hear their cause and pain,
which seems to help you let them go and free your heart again.
Now when your anger needs release, I trust the storm will pass;
once it's allowed to run its course it mostly doesn't last.

I realize that to stop its flow by thinking conflict's wrong,
just causes more frustration and the tension to prolong.
Where once I thought that angry feelings left us far apart
I now can see that staying with them opens up the heart.

So let's remember distance only grows when we avoid,
expressing angry feelings frees the passions once enjoyed.

HOLD THE ROPE

He baited and switched, and after
they hitched, seemed angry and dissatisfied.
She got frustrated, but it abated
once she sensed what he had inside.
As she suspected, he blindly
elected she'd be his true Mrs. Right.
Then his emotion gave him the notion
that caused him to want to take flight.

Love had awoken all that was broken
within him that had lied concealed.
They sought help needed, and then
succeeded to bring forth what had to be healed.
Some say that marriage, though it's
disparaged can serve to promote each one's growth.
'For better or worse', is not empty verse,
but a vow that's upheld by both.

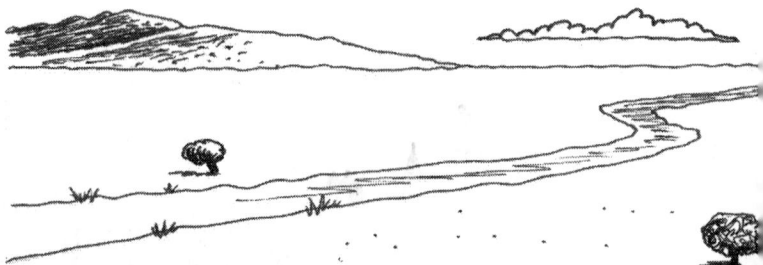

So during tough times when
growth's a steep climb, and
marriage needs us to cope,
Each partner may need
the other to lead,
and take their turn
holding the rope.

TILL DEATH DO US PART?

"To have and to hold until death do us part":
Great concept in theory, sounds fine at the start.
But during the years, as a marriage matures,
working things out and not heading for doors,
requires a challenge that's first not conceived,
where once there was lightness and what you believed
would be yours for the rest of your life.

But don't call the lawyers just yet if you find
that tempers prevail, love's no longer blind.
Not feeling the love doesn't mean that it's lost,
but fixing your problems may come at a cost.
You may not believe that there is a way out
when earlier efforts just led you to shout
and proclaim that the marriage is dead.

Find someone to help you, and bury you pride,
we've all been in your shoes, all torn up inside.
You may just not see it, because it's too close:
the problems you're having have been had by most.

Yet when it's in your yard the grass looks all brown,
so just make the effort while you're both around,
and hold off on having to part.

As much as it's tempting to give up and walk,
The very best outcomes begin when you talk.

MAKE THAT CHANGE

Namaste. I hope your day
Is filled with joy and stays that way.
But should it take a turn for worse,
and then you find you want to curse.
Seek tranquility inside.
'this too shall pass,' can be your guide.

Everything in life must change,
and should your life get rearranged.
Recall things are impermanent,
and try to change your temperament.
That's something that you can control—
So so make that change and peace your goal.

DÉJÀ VU?

Do you repeat and then react
to problems that you reenact?
Well if you do, and came to see
that there's another way to be,
you might just find that what transpires
comes like a phoenix out of fire,
rising again to recreate
familiar outcomes that you hate.

Is there a sense that there may be
a certain similarity,
to what you face again in life,
that brings familiar forms of strife?
Then look inside to find the key
for why you're so repeatedly
inclined to replicate and bear
effects from what you're unaware.

Tackle the monster; face the ghost
deal with that which scares you the most.
Get to the heart of what's not right,
or it will keep you up at night.

WE HERD

Our mind's made up. Our eyes are closed.
We believe what we hear.
We don't check its validity.
We're blinded by our fear.

We swear by false conspiracies
about outrageous deeds.
Despite their unrealities,
we follow where they lead.

Someday like frightened buffalo
they'll herd us off a cliff.
Then butchers with their knives below
will make our hides their gifts.

HERSTORY REPEATS

Mother Earth and all of her nations,
for ages have seen variations,
but most will repeat: war and defeat,
arising from man's degradations.

Many struggles get started by vices,
though leaders and nations deny this.
Then there's a war, which people abhor,
losing lives, because of the crisis.

Examine how most wars get started.
How ethics and virtue departed.
How power and greed and vanity lead,
how pride lust and wrath are imparted.

If we don't want the past to return,
then as humans we all need to learn,
to look deep within, and to slowly begin
shining light where our shadow's concerned.

"If you want to change the world, start with yourself."
—Mahatma Gandhi

A SPECIAL BURDEN

His quest was to be special, a burden it became.
A constant aspiration, a never-ending game.
Forbid that he be average, and not be singled out.
He had to show he's special, so all would stand and shout.

At times he thought he reached it, but soon it came to pass,
despite some fleeting glory, it never really last.
What drove this strong compulsion, a wound he couldn't soothe?
Compensatory Karma? Some thing he had to prove?

It surely had its downside, he couldn't quite 'just be.'
He became isolated, got lost in fantasy.
Who was he if not someone that stands out from the crowd?
The question asked, a wiser voice inside him said aloud:

"You are just one of many, one spoke upon the wheel.
Divine as much as others, compelled by what you feel.
You have your share of talents, and some you've yet to grow.
And doing so with friends you like, supports you as you go.

But if you need 'outstanding,' pursued all on your own,
then in your quest for specialness, you'll stand out, all alone."

BILLY'S NO G.O.A.T.

Billy was out at the plate
Rounded third just a little too late .
Should have stayed on that bag
Not ignored coach's flag
Just to do what he thought would be great.

He then got ignored by the team

For selfishly seeking his dream

Had he listened to coach

Running home not approached

The next batter hit in the seam.

His run would have won them the game

But the last out came round just the same

His team wound up losing

And he took to boozing

Now Billy's alone without fame.

UNITY

Buddha, Mohammed, Krishna, and Jesus
all took on missions where they sought to teach us.
It doesn't matter which land they were from,
and they wouldn't want us all to become
like fighting school children that argue who's dad
is bigger or better. That's virtually mad.
It's said, "Truth is one, but paths are many."
So find one that suits, instead of not any.

Don't polarize over the teachers who came.
They're spiritual leaders, each with his own name.
Stop finding the issues that drive us apart;
instead find compassion and love in your heart.
With hope and forgiveness, we'll all live in peace,
as brothers and sisters, and hatred will cease.
Division and conflict will always persist
until we seek unity and coexist.

WALKING A MINDFUL PATH

Though leaves have all fallen and branches are bare,
the floor of the forest may cover what's there.
Where some trees have toppled and partly decayed,
moss and dead foliage can hide where they're laid.

For hikers who tread on those hidden remains,
and fail to consider what's in such terrains,
they forge on assuming their footing is sound,
and sometimes get tripped up by what's underground.

The same thing can happen when unconsciously,
we get hurt in life by what we can't see.
When unresolved feelings repressed in our mind,
can cause us to suffer in ways where we're blind.

So if you seek traveling through life with less stress,
increase self-awareness and more mindfulness.

HOODS STOPPING BY
ON A SNOWY EVENING
(Black Lives Mattered, a parody)

Whose hoods these are I think I know.
Not from our village houses though.
I hope they won't be stopping here
to burn a cross and drape a bough.

My wife and son are filled with fear
that at our house they'll make it clear.
I spoke my mind and put at stake
my very life, the price I'll bear.

They pull their harness reins to break.
They're stopping here, there's no mistake.
I see this and feel terror creep.
My body's stiff, I start to shake.

Their eyes reveal an evil deep,
Where hatred and injustice keep.
No trials to go before I sleep.
No trials to go before I sleep.

SNOWFLAKES AND WATER

Snowflakes and water—they differ but all share
the same basic essence as one.
We too are unique, and multitudes speak
in languages with foreign tongues.

Yet we're linked in spirit, so trust when you hear it,
have faith and you'll come to agree.
Because disbelievers would have us conceive there's
no truth in such world unity.

And there are some nations who seek separation
and think that's the way it should be.
They restrain their countries, don't let people live free,
they're threatened by what they can't see.

You must function their way, live life how they say,
support how their governments run;
This causes frictions, conflicting convictions,
conditions where wars are begun.

We need free relations, not jailed populations,
that only lead people to fight.
We each want to live life in peace, without strife,
a spirit where we all unite.

That spirit pervades us, surrounds us, and made us,
it created all that exists.
God is its highest, and though some deny this,
they have the born right to resist.

If peace is our goal, then we must accept all,
keep tolerance close in our hearts.
So let's not surrender to forces that render
oppression and drive us apart.

THREE EYES OF THE SOUL

To truly know an apple can't just only be in thought.
You'll need all of your senses if its wholeness is what's sought.
To see, to smell, to taste a bite,
to hold it in your hand, to hear it snap
between your teeth is what it will demand.

If told a vase of fragile glass had dropped upon a stone,
the logical conclusion that it shattered could be known.
There are realities in life that logic can deduce,
yet some things need objective
proof where facts can be produced.

But knowing if a God exists evades objective sense,
and logical analysis won't do for evidence.
It's contemplation that provides the way His truth is known.
It opens up your consciousness so that His truth is shown.

CONCENTRATION, MEDITATION, CONTEMPLATION

These three mental practices often get confused,
but they can work together, each one can be used
to orient and focus, to settle down your mind,
and give you opportunity to get yourself aligned.

To enter meditation you first must concentrate,
be conscious of your breathing, and mindfully abate
distracting thoughts and feelings, so that you can begin,
contemplating all the truths arising from within.

Gaining such an outcome takes practice and takes time.
Patience is required, but results can be sublime.
Persevere and don't give up even if you're tired.
Have faith and trust this method is a way to get inspired.

RATTLED TO INSIGHT

I had a dream so frightening it jolted me awake.
I found myself out walking through a path with lots of snakes.
They filled the ground, were all
around, I wanted to get through.
I tried to step between them, but the spaces were so few.

While some snakes slumbered
undisturbed, some others slithered by,
but then one rattled suddenly and raised its head up high.
Positioning itself to strike, I then abruptly woke.
My heart was pounding, and
my sweat had made my pillow soak.

I laid there thinking if I could arrive at some insight,
because I've had that dream
before which wakes me up at night.
It seems to come from time to time, I want to find a key,
to learn what it may symbolize, what I may need to see.

As I reflected through the night, awareness came with dawn.
I realized that this dream occurs
when I fear something's wrong.

I further came to recognize when my fears get denied,
they rise up from the darker places where they tend to hide.

But when acknowledged and
addressed, my dreams can help me see,
what's down in my unconscious that is calling out to me.

MYSTIC'S PRAYER

Now I lay me down to sleep,
I pray my spirit lets me reap
the gifts that I possess inside,
subconsciously where they reside.
While in this zone of consciousness
with theta waves and mind at rest,
I pray my brain will soon transmit,
what's supernormal, and emit
the higher gifts of functioning,
capacities I've yet to bring
to my awareness consciously,
endowed to all humanity.
But should I sleep before I find
these vast potentials of my mind,
I pray that on some future night
my spirit brings them into sight.

"OH WORTHY, AWAKE!"

"Oh worthy, awake!" When I hear that it makes
me intend to become more aware,
of what lies inside where my spirit resides,
out of sight, but is ever so near.

It's not body-bound, but is where it is found
if awareness is made to expand.
In order to see its unique subtlety
my perception must widen its band.

Like a forgotten dream where images seem
to retreat from my memory bank,
my spiritual sight and the dreams during night
seem to hide where awareness is blank.

It's quite hard to say why they covertly lay
out of sight, but I'd sure like to know.
If what they conceal, what I think or I feel,
will reveal just how I need to grow.

As Emerson said, all of what lies ahead,
or behind are comparatively,
of tiny concern; it's inside where we learn
intuitions that offer the Key.

When it is found, you'll be on sacred ground
with a sense of God's kingdom within.
So direct your focus inside to your locus.
Awaken to what's always been.

PARALYZED BY PERFECTION

We're paralyzed by our perfection,
can't even get out of the gate.
Won't start off in any direction,
until we're assured we'll be great.
We set the bar high, and don't
realize the struggle may be worth the fuss.
We're frozen by fear, and think
what lies ahead is a failure for us.

But failing can lead to new learning,
and show where we need to improve.
And yes, it's a hard way of earning
the wisdom of which way to move.
It's fine if we have high ambition.
Seek the sun, but just reach the moon.
At least we'll move on with our mission,
not regret we gave up too soon.

So when we pursue inspirations,
perseverance is what's required.
Remember creative inventions,
were produced by those who perspired.

EYE PHONES

If your lifeline is your smartphone,
then you've found what's widely known:
The many ways you can connect
with everyone, and collect
extensive knowledge where it lies,
instantly before your eyes.

Yet there are downsides you won't see,
if increased dependency,
should lead you to become withdrawn,
always focused on your phone.

While you may say there's nothing wrong.
All is well, you'll get along.
There will be times it will distract
your attention where it's lacked.
And while your head is looking down,
you may miss what's all around,
or not see that which lies within,
creative thoughts that begin
a path to great discoveries,
like smartphones, or what can be.

GOLDILOCKS' STILLACTION

Sometimes it's clear to see, we need to let things be.
And when it's time to act, proceed assertively.
But when it's not so clear, which tack will likely bear
results we seek to gain, or outcomes that we fear.
To know which way to choose, the best approach to use,
requires vigilance and recognizing cues.

Yet insecurity can raise anxiety,
and prompt us much too soon, to act impulsively.
So despite what we feel, know when to remain still,
when things can't be controlled or overcome by will.
And know when we may stay accepting and resigned,
where change calls us to act, yet we're just not inclined.

Cause obstacles can lift, and like a sudden gift,
blow wind into our sails, when we feel stalled adrift.
If then we have a plan to implement which can
be done if we're not still. The time to act's at hand.

One day we'll learn from growth how we can balance both;
not acting premature, nor falling prey to sloth.

KUNDALINI RIVER

River rise through me, your current be strong.

Rouse my creations, inspire a song.

Surge up my centers and fill chakras' crown.

Clear away fears as you flow all around.

Fears clog my mind up like boulders and trees

disrupt your flowing, so I ask you please,

also to guide me where deep pools reside,

then in your stillness, it's where I'll abide.

GETTING OFF THE WHEEL

He lived lives lost and longing, passed years in quite despair.
In one he held much power and made his subjects fear.
Another found him panicked running home to find surprised
that all those loved around him were killed and brutalized.

He lived once as a black man, strung up for speaking out.
And one time as a child abused, he felt great shame and doubt.
One life he was a soldier with victory well in hand,
who struck down helpless peasants fleeing in a band.

A monk in France he threatened the beliefs held by the church.
His feet and hands tied to a post,
he burned because he searched.
Those lives and many others he retrieved have shown him how,
impressions branded on his soul can influence him now.

But beyond all the insights that were gained from his review,
he learned how karmic balancing requires lives renew.

WE'RE SELF-CLEANING OVENS

We're self-cleaning ovens that burn off the seeds
of karma compiled from all our past deeds.
The good and bad outcomes that balance the sheet,
are repaid by sowing the fates that we meet.
There's no outside agent to blame for effects
from lifetimes of causes. Our conscience elects
the ways we evolve to master and grow,
so we'll gain the wisdom to then truly know
that we are empowered to create what seems
like heaven or hell on this earth from our dreams.

WHO'S DRIVING THE BUS?

When weighing right or wrong it's wise
to let your conscience guide,
but sometimes it gets compromised
by what you feel inside.
Because there's times you know what's right,
but choose the other way,
attracted by that small delight,
the urge to disobey.

You certainly won't be the first
whose shadow took the wheel,
and drove your life into reverse,
because of what you feel.
We all can become victimized
by our unconscious drives,
where what's repressed is not realized
and undermines our lives.

The antidote that will ensure
that you don't blindly choose
to wander off and then explore
directions where you lose,
is know when you're conflicted
and recognize you must
be sure that you've elected
your conscience drives the bus.

"A NOTE FROM ST. PETER, C.P.A."

I'm anally compulsive: cross t's and dot my i's
I take the loose from Lucifer, distill things down to size.
There're many deeds upon this earth that you may someday do,
but when you're at my pearly gates I'll surely audit you.

Accounting for the details, where all your deeds are known,
I'll log them in a ledger, so they'll be clearly shown.
There'll be a precise record of everything on file,
and when it's time to judge your life, it all will reconcile.

So keep in mind all that you do gets sent up to my cloud,
where I weigh what you've done
that's good, and what is not allowed.
And Santa's' not the only one who brings you gifts or coal.
I Ho-Ho-Hope that you've been good so this won't take a toll.

IS IT REALLY TOO LATE FOR YOU?

Are you sure that it's too late for you,
to do what you once meant to do?
Dreams that you courted, but since aborted,
because you think your life is through?

Reassess and take a deep breath.
If you're actually not close to death.
There may be no limit, just your fears
that transmit the thought that
there is no time left.

If once all those dreams in your bucket,
were thrown out and you just said: "Fuck it!"
Should life still have fruit that draws your pursuit,
why not reach out and go pluck it?

Now is the time to consider,
not waste precious days while you dither.
Don't grow complacent with how your day's spent,
realize those dreams and don't wither.

A RAINY DAY DEMISE

Rain down the day of my demise,
but not to tear my griever's eyes.
Assuage my parting consciousness
from any fears I may possess.

Pelt down your drops with pounding splats.
Implode my ears with rat-a-tats.
Distract my mind as body's grip
allows my spirits' subtle slip.

Through doors ajar and windows wide,
impose your sound of rain inside.
And let the constant falling stream
escort me from this latest dream.

No need for thoughts or anxious breath
about existence after death.
Continued life my faith believes,
like winter trees without their leaves.

Though seasons change, the earth renews,
and much that lives is out of view.
The leaves return, and I will too,
to live again with more to do.

So in your flow let me unfurl
from loosened knots, and like a pearl
that's finally freed from off its string,
I'll glide away to spirits' spring.

THE BACK VIEW

Tree line clear

Mountain blues

Setting sun on river's face

Reflecting

Rusty swings

Widows' weeds

Fallen limbs on family tree

Recalling

Overgrowth

In retreat

Floodplain in my eye line view

Perspective

Dog and I see

ACKNOWLEDGEMENTS

Special thanks go to Michael Grosso, David Waters, Jane Pasciuti, and Patrick Huyghe for their extensive editing, contributions, and encouragement. A big thank you to my talented illustrator, Craig M. Linderman, who skillfully captured the images of a select number of poems.

And an additional thanks to those who read the early versions of the poems and provided valuable feedback: Kevin McFadden, Steve Sayre, Renee Shacochis, Eric Pasciuti, Michelle Yentsch, and Joe Connor.

Finally, much appreciation to Laura Smyth at Smythtype Design, who structured and prepared this book for publishing.

Also by Frank Pasciuti, Ph.D.

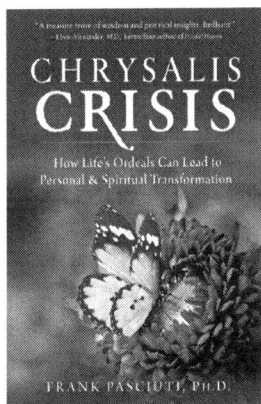

Recovering from a life ordeal—be it the death of a loved one, a divorce, loss of a job, or a serious physical injury or sickness—can sometimes result in personal and spiritual growth. When it does, Dr. Frank Pasciuti calls the transformative experience a "Chrysalis Crisis." If properly managed, these kinds of crises can result in increased physical, emotional, intellectual, social, and moral development.

Using stories from his clients and his personal life, Dr. Pasciuti shows how a Chrysalis Crisis can prompt growth in ten key areas of human functioning. It can awaken our very real capacity for psychic abilities and deeply enhance our spiritual lives. This book offers a model of human development that enables everyone—not just those in crises—to transform their lives, and create for themselves an increased sense of peace, happiness, and well-being.

"A treasure trove of wisdom and practical insights. Brilliant!"
—Eben Alexander, MD, bestselling author of *Proof of Heaven*

Made in the USA
Middletown, DE
18 November 2024